Crafting with Nature

FROM ROOT TO STEM

Science and Craft Projects with Seeds and Plants

By Ruth Owen

Enslow PUBLISHING

Published in 2024 by Enslow Publishing, LLC
2544 Clinton Street
Buffalo, NY 14224

Portions of this work were originally authored by Ruth Owen and published as *Science and Craft Projects with Plants and Seeds*. All new material this edition authored by Ruth Owen.

Produced for Rosen by Ruby Tuesday Books Ltd
Editor for Ruby Tuesday Books Ltd: Mark J. Sachner
Designer: Emma Randall

Manufactured in the United States of America

CPSIA compliance information: Batch #CSENS24: For further information contact
Enslow Publishing LLC, New York, New York at 1-800-398-2504.

Please visit our website, www.enslowpublishing.com. For a free color catalog of all our high-quality books,
call toll free 1-800-398-2504 or fax 1-877-980-4454.

Cataloging-in-Publication Data

Names: Owen, Ruth.
Title: From root to stem: science and craft projects with seeds and plants / Ruth Owen.
Description: New York : Enslow Publishing, 2024. | Series: Crafting with nature | Includes glossary and index.
Identifiers: ISBN 9781978535572 (pbk.) | ISBN 9781978535589 (library bound) | ISBN 9781978535596 (ebook)
Subjects: LCSH: Nature craft--Juvenile literature.
Classification: LCC TT160.O94 2024 | DDC 745.5--dc23

Photo Credits:
Cover, 1, 4–5, 6, 7, 8–9, 10–11, 14–15, 16–17, 18, 20–21, 22–23, 24, 25 (top), 26–27 © Shutterstock;
12–13, 25 (bottom), 28–29 © Ruby Tuesday Books Ltd; 19 © Wikipedia Creative Commons.

CONTENTS

A WORLD OF PLANTS

There are plants in gardens, parks, and forests. They also survive in **habitats** such as hot, dry **deserts** and the cold, windy Arctic **tundra**.

Scientists have studied and named more than 390,000 different types of plants—from tall trees to tiny wildflowers such as dandelions.

a dandelion

Inside this book, you will find out lots of facts about plants. You can also learn how some plants **reproduce**, or make new plants, by growing **seeds.** There are also six fun plant craft projects to make!

Saving Water, Keeping Warm

Saguaro cacti grow in a desert habitat where very little rain falls. If it does rain, a saguaro sucks up water through its roots and stores it in its fleshy stems. Pasqueflowers grow on the Arctic tundra. These plants are covered with hairs as protection against the cold.

pasqueflower

PLANT PARTS IN ACTION

The different parts of a plant all have important jobs to do.

Plants suck up water and **nutrients** from the soil through their roots.

A plant's roots grow down into the soil and hold a plant steady so it doesn't fall over. Roots can be as thin as a hair or thicker than a person's arm!

A plant's main stem grows from its roots and connects to thinner stems. The stems carry water and nutrients from the roots to the rest of the plant.

Some plants have flowers where the plants' seeds are made.

The World's Biggest Flower

The plant with the biggest flower in the world is the *Rafflesia arnoldii*. Rafflesias grow in rain forests on the Asian islands of Borneo and Sumatra. The flower of the *Rafflesia arnoldii* can grow to be 3 feet (1 m) wide!

FOREVER FLOWERS

Freshly picked flowers may only last for a few days. But if you press them inside the pages of a heavy book, they will dry out and will be preserved forever!

GET CRAFTING:

You will need:
- Fresh flowers and leaves
- Waxed paper
- One large, heavy book
- Several other heavy books
- Colorful construction paper or thin cardboard
- An adult to be your teammate and go flower hunting with you
- Glue

1. Before you gather your flowers and leaves, make sure you ask permission from the person who owns the plants. If you cannot pick flowers in a garden you can use store-bought flowers instead.

2. Pick some flower heads and leaves that look fresh and colorful. Make sure the flowers are not wet when you pick them. Go onto step 3 as quickly as possible so the flowers are as fresh as possible when you press them.

3 Place the large, heavy book on a flat surface and open it. Lay a piece of waxed paper on the right-hand page.

4 Lay some flowers and leaves on the waxed paper.

5 Cover the flowers with another sheet of waxed paper. Then close the book.

6 Now open the book in another place and repeat steps 3 to 5. Keep doing this until you have used up all your flowers and leaves.

7 Put the heavy book in a place where it will not be disturbed, and put the other books on top of it to add weight.

8 Now comes the waiting part! You will need to wait for two weeks. In that time, the flowers will dry out and become flat, so you can use them to make pictures.

9 When it's time to look at your flowers, carefully open the pages of the book. The flowers will be delicate, so handle them carefully.

10 Glue the pressed flowers and leaves to construction paper or cardboard to make pictures and greetings cards.

ALL ABOUT POLLINATION

In order for a flower to make seeds it must be **pollinated.** This important task is often carried out with the help of insects, birds, and other small animals.

Flowers produce a dust called **pollen** on their **anthers.**

When an animal, such as a bee or butterfly, visits a flower, some pollen sticks to the animal's body.

Then the bee flies off and visits a different flower of the same kind. Some of the pollen on the animal's body brushes off and sticks to that flower's **stigma.**

The flower with pollen on its stigma is now pollinated and can begin to make seeds.

Pollinators

Animals that move pollen from flower to flower on their bodies are called pollinators. Insects such as bees, butterflies, and beetles are pollinators. So are some types of birds and bats. Most pollinators visit flowers to feed on a sweet liquid called nectar that flowers produce.

a hummingbird drinking nectar

BUSY BUG CLIPS

In summer, try to find a butterfly that's flying from flower to flower, drinking nectar. Then see if you can spot the little insect's long tongue dipping in and out of the flowers. Celebrate these busy little insects by making these fun clips made from wooden clothespins.

You will need

- Wooden clothespins
- Colorful construction paper or thin cardboard
- Scissors
- Colored markers or pens
- Glue
- Pipe cleaners
- Peel-and-stick goggly eyes
- An adult to be your teammate and help with cutting

GET CRAFTING:

1. Draw the shape of four wings on the cardboard or construction paper. Ask an adult to help you cut them out.

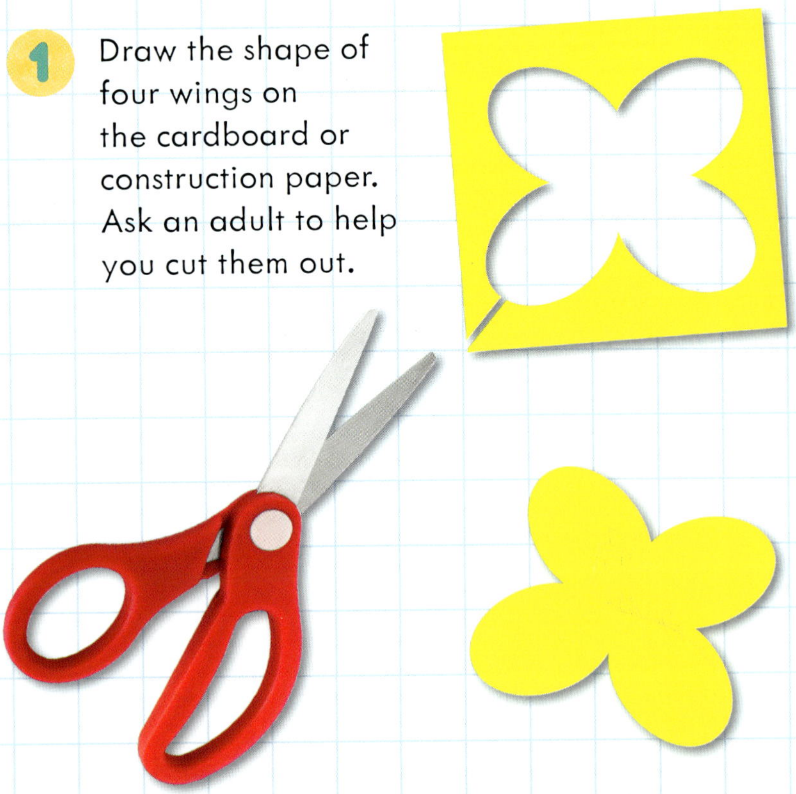

2. Decorate the wings with spots, stripes, or other patterns.

3 Glue the wings to the back of a wooden clothespin.

4 Draw stripes, spots, or other patterns on the clothespin to make the butterfly's body.

5 Bend a pipe cleaner into a V shape. Then bend the ends into spirals to make the butterfly's antennae. Glue the antennae between the two halves of the clothespin.

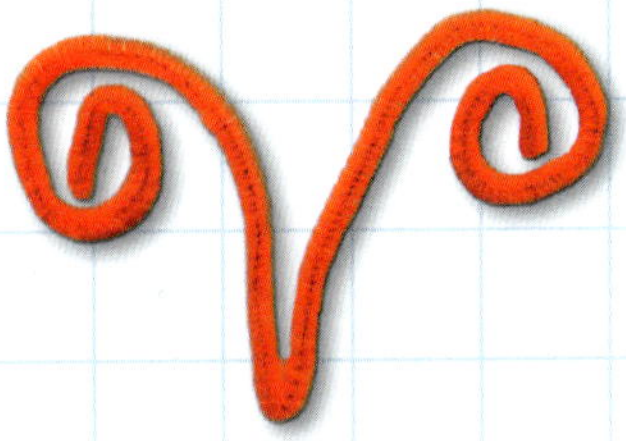

6 Stick the goggly eyes to the butterfly's head.

7 Your butterfly clip is ready to use to hold photographs or important messages. You can also make butterfly clips to give as gifts!

FRUITS AND SEEDS

A flower's main job is to make seeds that will become new plants. After a flower has been pollinated, seeds start to form inside the flower.

A flowering plant's seeds grow inside a protective case, or covering, called a fruit.

dying flower

a poppy seedpod, or fruit

poppy flower

a dried poppy seedpod, or fruit

poppy seeds

The seeds can be as small as specks of dust or as big as a table tennis ball.

You might think of a fruit as being an apple or a peach. A fruit, however, is any kind of outer layer that protects seeds as they grow.

Some fruits, such as melons, tomatoes, or bean pods, are soft. Others, such as acorns, are hard. Inside an acorn is a seed that can grow into a new oak tree.

Seeds from Cones

Plants without flowers grow their seeds in other ways. Pine trees grow their seeds inside cones. When the seeds are fully grown, the pine cone's scales open up so the seeds can fall out.

HANDPRINT SUNFLOWER

A sunflower is a large, beautiful flower that can produce about 1,000 seeds in its center. In this fun project, you can make a handprint sunflower decorated with real seeds in its center.

You will need:

- Yellow finger paint
- A flat dish or container
- Large sheet of white construction paper
- Scissors
- A saucer
- A pencil
- Glue (choose a clear glue)
- A piece of black cardboard approximately 10 inches by 10 inches (25 cm x 25 cm)
- Sunflower seeds in shells or kernels
- An adult to be your teammate and help with cutting

GET CRAFTING:

1. Ask an adult to help you pour the paint into the flat container.

2. On the large piece of construction paper, make 10 or 12 paint handprints. When the handprints are dry, ask an adult to help you cut out them out.

3 Place the saucer upside down on the black cardboard and draw around it with the pencil. Ask an adult to help you cut out the circle you have made.

4 Now glue the handprints behind the circle of black cardboard so they look like a sunflower's petals.

5 Carefully spread glue all over the black center of the sunflower.

6 Sprinkle lots of sunflower seeds over the glue. Press the seeds into the glue and make sure there are no gaps between the seeds.

7 You now have a beautiful, seed-packed sunflower to hang on your wall!

This real sunflower has died and lost its petals. You can see the seeds in the flower's center.

HOW DOES A SEED GROW?

Once a seed has formed, it is ripe and ready to find a place to grow. For example, when the seedpods on a bean plant split open, the bean seeds fall from the parent plant.

Most seeds ripen in summer and fall. Once they are settled in some soil, they wait for spring before starting to grow. First, roots grow from the seed into the soil. Then a shoot, or seedling, grows aboveground.

The seedling has been taking water and nutrients from the soil through its little roots. Now it also needs sunlight to grow. Soon, tiny leaves sprout from the seedling. Then the seedling grows and grows to become a plant.

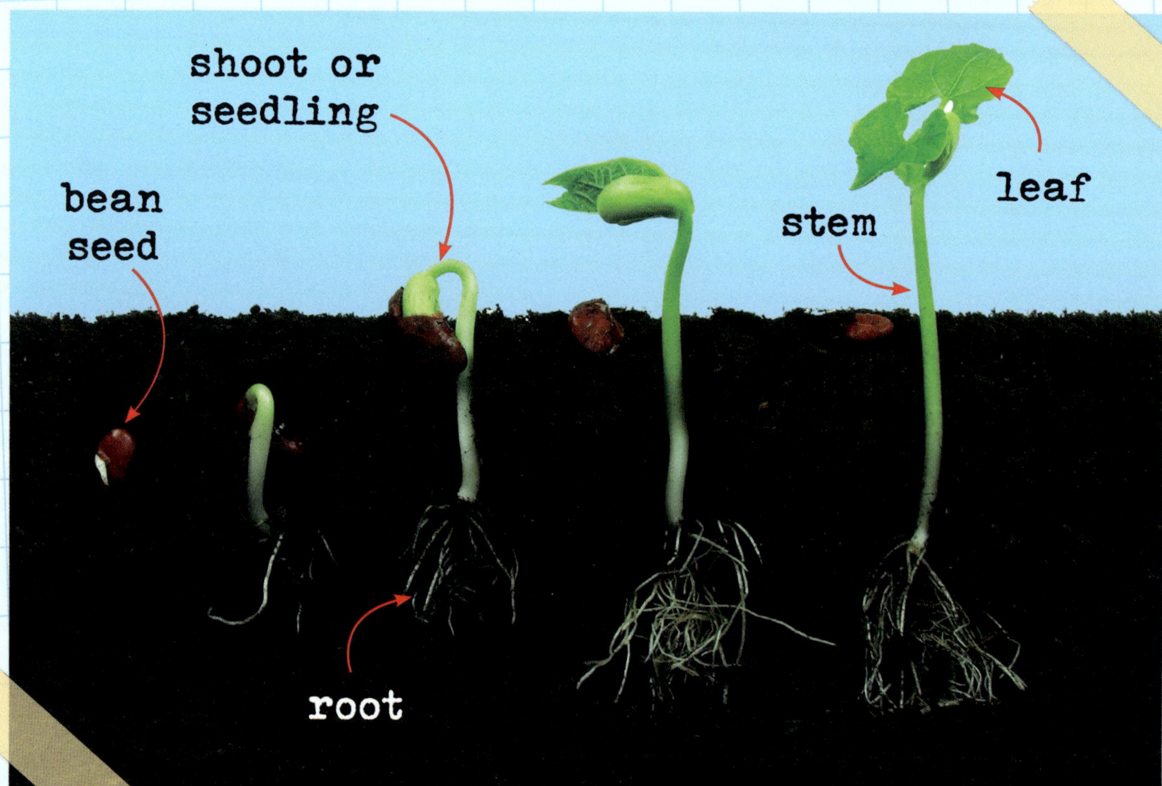

Tiny Seeds, Giant Plants

Redwood trees are the tallest plants in the world. A redwood seed, however, is not much bigger than a grain of rice. It takes hundreds of years, but a tiny seed may grow into a redwood tree that is as tall as a 30-story building!

SUPER SEEDS ARTWORK

Seeds grow in many different colors and shapes which makes them a great material to use to create art. All it takes to make a beautiful seed picture is some cardboard, glue, and lots of colorful seeds.

You will need:

- A selection of dried seeds
- Small bowls
- Black or white thin cardboard
- A pencil
- Glue (choose a clear glue)

GET CRAFTING:

1. Put all your different seeds into individual bowls.

green peas

yellow split peas

red kidney beans

chickpeas

pinto beans

black beans

broad beans

red lentils

2. Decide what type of picture you want to make. You can write your name, create a landscape scene, or make patterns.

3 First, draw your design on a piece of cardboard.

4 Spread glue in a small section of your picture. Sprinkle seeds over the glue so that the whole section is thickly covered with seeds.

5 Now spread glue in another section. Keep working on your picture section by section.

6 Once you've finished your picture, leave it lying flat until the glue has completely dried. Have fun!

7 You can draw shapes and fill them with different seeds to make patterns (like the circle below). You can even make a seed mosaic frame for a favorite photograph.

A LITTLE SEED'S NEW HOME

Once a seed is ready to grow, it must find a growing place away from its parent plant. Why?

If a seed tries to grow in the soil close to its parent plant, there may not be enough water and nutrients to go around. The bigger plant may also block out the sunlight. Therefore, it makes sense for a tiny seed to find a new place to grow.

Some seeds get moved to new places in the stomachs of animals!

A bird might eat some berries or other fruit with seeds inside. Then the bird will fly off to a new place with the seeds in its stomach. The seeds will be released into the new place with the bird's waste.

A horse with burdock seeds stuck in its mane.

Some seeds are sticky or prickly. These seeds can become attached to the fur of animals and get carried to a new place to grow.

Flying seeds

Dandelion seeds are blown to new growing places by the wind. Each seed is attached to a tiny, fluffy parachute that catches the wind and helps the seed float away from its parent plant.

DANDELION SEEDS PAINTING

A dandelion flower can produce up to 200 fluffy, flying seeds. Using paint and wax, you can create a lovely painting of a dandelion spreading its seeds.

You will need:
- White paper
- Paint
- Paintbrushes
- A white wax crayon
- A black marker
- A magnifying glass

GET CRAFTING:

1. Before you start on your artwork, take a close look at the dandelion seed head in this picture. Better still, if it is spring, summer, or fall, try to find a real dandelion seed head.

2 Try using a magnifying glass to study a dandelion's tiny black seeds and their fluffy parachutes.

3 To make your picture, draw a fluffy dandelion seed head with the white crayon. Draw the fluffy parachute parts of the seeds floating in the air, too.

4 With the black marker, add black dots for seeds attached to each of the parachutes.

5 Now comes the really amazing part. Cover the whole picture with blue paint. The wax will resist, or throw off, the paint and the areas on the paper where you drew the dandelions in crayon will remain white!

6 You can try different designs using this effect. For example, use the crayon to draw lots of dandelions on the ground and white, fluffy clouds in the sky.

PLANTS FOR SURVIVAL

Without plants, people and animals could not survive. Many of the foods we eat such as fruits, vegetables, seeds, and rice come from plants.

Grains such as wheat are grass plants that we use to make flour. Delicious foods such as bread, cakes, cookies, and pancakes are all made from flour.

You might think you could survive by eating only hamburgers or sausage. These foods would not exist without plants, however. That's because meat comes from plant-eating animals such as cattle and pigs.

No Ice Cream Without Plants!

Without plants, we wouldn't have milk, or foods made from milk such as cheese and ice cream. That's because we get milk from dairy cows or goats that eat grass and other plants. It's possible to make milk in other ways, but not without plants. Soy milk and rice milk are both made from plants!

PRINTING WITH PRODUCE

Fruits and vegetables have great shapes that look good on our plates, but they can also be used for printing! In this project, give a T-shirt a colorful new plant-based look by printing with veggies and fruits, such as corn, apples, and pieces of broccoli.

You will need:

- A plain T-Shirt
- Fabric paints (ask an adult to read the packaging of the fabric paint to check if there are any special instructions before you begin work)
- Dishes (one for each paint color)
- Paintbrushes
- Your choice of fruits and vegetables
- A cutting board
- A knife
- Paper
- An adult to be your teammate and help with cutting the fruits and vegetables

GET CRAFTING:

1. Pour the paints into the dishes.

2. Now ask an adult to help you cut up the fruits and vegetables. To create a design on your T-shirt, you will be dipping the pieces of fruits and vegetables into the paints.

3. Try out some ideas and designs on paper before you begin work on your T-shirt.

4. Once you have decided on a design, get crafty on your T-shirt. Dip a piece of fruit or vegetable into the paint, or use a paintbrush to cover it with paint. Then press the shape onto the fabric.

5. When you have finished your design, allow the paint to dry. Then follow any special final instructions on the packaging of the fabric paint.

Fruits such as apples, oranges, and lemons can be cut in half to make patterns like this.

Pieces of broccoli make pretty, fluffy patterns.

Trim off the base of a romaine lettuce. Its pattern looks like a flower.

Put pieces of corn onto skewers. These can be rolled onto paper or fabric.

GLOSSARY

anther (AN-thur)
The part of a flower that produces pollen.

desert (DEH-zurt)
A dry, rocky, or sandy habitat where very little rain or snow falls and few plants can grow. Some deserts are very hot, while others are very cold.

habitat (HA-buh-tat)
The place where an animal or plant normally lives. A habitat may be a backyard, a forest, the ocean, or a pond in a park.

nutrients (NOO-tree-ents)
Substances needed by a plant or animal to help it live and grow. Animals get nutrients, such as vitamins, from their food, while plants get nutrients from the soil.

pollen (PAH-lin)
A colored dust made on the anthers of flowers, which plants need in order to reproduce.

pollinated (PAH-luh-nayt-ed)
When pollen is carried from the anthers of a flower to the stigma. Pollen can be moved between these parts on the same plant or to a different plant of the same kind.

reproduce (ree-pruh-DOOS)
To make more of something, such as when plants make seeds or animals mate in order to produce young.

ripe (RYP)
Fully grown and ready to leave a parent plant.

seed (SEED)
A part of a plant that contains all the material needed to grow a new plant.

stigma (STIG-muh)
The part, or parts, of a flower where pollen must land in order for pollination to happen so that a flower can begin to make seeds.

tundra (TUN-druh)
The frozen land of the coldest parts of the world.

Websites

https://www.firstpalette.com/craft-theme/flowers-plants.html

https://kids.kiddle.co/Plant

https://www.fs.usda.gov/wildflowers/pollinators/animals/index.shtml

Publisher's note to parents and teachers: Our editors have reviewed the websites listed here to make sure they're suitable for students. However, websites may change frequently. Please note that students should always be supervised when they access the internet.

READ MORE

Bolte, Mari. *How Plants Will Save the World (STEM to the Rescue)*. Minneapolis, MN: Full Tilt Press, 2023.

Griffin, Mary. *Stinky Corpse Flowers (Fantastic Plants)*. New York, NY: Rosen Publishing, 2023.

Owen, Ruth. *Let's Investigate How Trees Grow (Get Started with STEM)*. Minneapolis, MN: Ruby Tuesday Books, 2022.

INDEX